Free Verse Editions

Edited by Jon Thompson

SUNSHINE WOUND

L. S. KLATT

Parlor Press
Anderson, South Carolina
www.parlorpress.com

Parlor Press LLC, Anderson, South Carolina, 29621

Printed in the United States of America
S A N: 2 5 4 - 8 8 7 9

Library of Congress Cataloging-in-Publication Data on File

Cover design by Don Hettinga.
Cover art: "Wild Flowers," by Kathleen Lolley. Used by
permission of the artist.

Printed on acid-free paper.

Parlor Press, LLC is an independent publisher of scholarly and
trade titles in print and multimedia formats. This book is available
in paperback and ebook formats from Parlor Press on the World
Wide Web at http://www.parlorpress.com or through online and
brick-and-mortar bookstores. For submission information or to
find out about Parlor Press publications, write to Parlor Press,
3015 Brackenberry Drive, Anderson, South Carolina, 29621, or
email editor@parlorpress.com.

For Kathleen McCarthy, 1961-2011,
friend who knew both sun and wound

Contents

A not admitting of the wound
Until it grew so wide...

—*Emily Dickinson*

SUNSHINE WOUND

Intrepid Pilot

Dear Stranger, if a lark chased by birdshot
seeks asylum where things are hidden, go
to it with an armload of chameleons &
armadillos. And if, in the flooded glades
of the Orinoco, you discover a woman
bathing a panther with lilac oils, go to her.
And if you eavesdrop on certain light-
bearing insects, take a bicycle that will wheel
you into dark space. What you must not
blot out, but rather imagine, is that your cloak
is a lifeboat. Into midnight then fall backward
because, weightless there, you phosphoresce
in a slipstream of transit.

Sanctuary

There's something burning
in the thicket. I run to it
with a recorder at first
blush of indigo. The pair
of buntings netted in brambles;
I hear their cries; I want
their wounds. Is life
worth living? Maybe;
the hidden life. The bower
seems another guidebook
with green leaves. So as
Ulysses S. Grant is folded
in my wallet, I will go
intrepidly into thicket;
for U.S. has engulfed me
but not consumed me.

Dooms of Balm

The earth is covered
in lilacs. Corals
in the lilac sea mean
brains are thinking
of bee balm. When
deadheads

last perfumed, there was a purple discharge, then
a gratitude. We sleep, knowing we may be ambushed

by a lilac dream,
but the sun is
a friend, our ultra-
violet friend. To
make a synthetic
grief out of lilacs
is not to feel
purposeless.

F♮

Every now & then, when the mind is on f
ire, I soak it in an ice bath of music. Or go out in a squall o
f soft metal blossoms f
rom a soft metal tree. I mean, of course, the lithium tree. And i
f, as I go, I get in my car & drive, avoiding a runner & her tiptop legs, a f
aulty battery is enough to propel me. "Where are you?" I ask o
f myself.

You Create a World Then Live in that World

The blue palm of the firmament holds the Flatiron
like a honeycomb. The Flatiron is weighted with sunshine,
as is the future. And why wouldn't the palm

throw a shadow as it positions & repositions the Flatiron?
The honeycomb in the crotch of Manhattan;
the Flatiron on a shirttail. It is dress-up day. The tulips

droop like goosenecks. The blue palm is scarred
by airliners. The commuters, fork-tender, pass each other
with little regard. Goodbye, yes, eyes of yesterday.

Knickerbocker

Suppose a man steps out of the fog
to meet us. And suppose, having just left
his deathbed, he arrives wearing a suit
of blank checks, & it's not so bad—
the paper trail is brilliant, & it smells like the New
York Stock Exchange. And let that man
give fair warning under a buttonwood tree
& broker for us the underworld. And if
all he shares is traded, let the man
in his essence be a number, & if a number
a sign, & if a sign, let him be heeded.
But suppose the man leaves one foot in the grave
& reaches out to us not with a foghorn
but a what if.

The Head of George Washington

The head of George Washington, largely forgotten except for portraits
where the face is powdered, the cheeks rosy, & excluding busts
on which phrenologists have digressed, lies under a cherry tree.

The snow has gone to ridiculous lengths to conceal it, but his aquiline
nose is a telltale sign that the globe is warming. And truly the seven icebergs,
like wise men, wander from their calving to approach the sweet lips

of the revolutionary. In their quiet way, the bergs describe a journey
over gridlock into a heretofore unimaginable cloudburst, which melts them
& makes them seem like Holsteins grazing on hilltops. Into the valley, the seven

verge, keeping an eye out for monuments & rivers of children,
while the head, ensconced in fallen fruit, looks like it wants to speak.

St. Louis

Thus grew the aftermath where so-and-so
had a feeling of if. The white crow had been befogged

as it ate out the eyes of a possum, &, while the woodpeckers
were whacking away at elm trees, roadside, it went on asking itself

what it now knew. The crow was a constant thing
in a brownfield puddled with standing water. And one might

rhapsodize, as spring carried on, of the whiteness
losing its novelty. So-and-so could have spent a lifetime

descrying what might have been. So-and-so could have been
a huckleberry looking west of Mizzou.

St. Francis

I carry a calf in my hand. It has a handle
& a secret compartment. I set it down
in an amphitheater where the New
Romans assemble. They have ways
of caressing my livestock
though a little too familiar. I suspect
a wisdom lives in the hide of the calf
which requires a fetish. What is the cure
for an excessive love of animal?
The afterlife turns flesh to grass
& grass to cowslips; & there is always
the chance of a blue sky.

Painters on Our Way to Work

All of us have a dream power we are apt to forget,
remember dimly: the impasto on withering
things like fingers & legs. The scalloped sweat

of armpits on the shirt
of a man who wades
through fields, blade
by blade, must mean

that God also passes by, affected, like a brushstroke.
The sunlight can make us crazy; think of the gun
in the painter's smock as crows light on shocks of wheat.

Figure at Night Following Phosphorescent Tracks

Like petals of moonlight, snowflakes in their anomie. And I,
like my ancestor the moonwalker, fall & break my hip
under them.

It seems as if we spacemen enjoy our barrage of moonlight,
which we mangle with gloved hands, light that does not
resemble frostbite.

The good life that we seek is not a matter of affectation
or bravura; it is the moment when the hierophants
discover gravity.

For all the gaudiness of the good earth & the good moon
cannot, like the snow owl, lift up the heads
of the snowbound.

The indeterminate yield to a wilderness of lightness.

Bittern

I am against the death-wish, unless. Unless
the bittern, exposed to sight, stiffens. Or
some other odd bird, in service of life, mortifies.

A wish with green feet will build a watchtower among the loose-
strife.

What a horrible voice the wish has, feigning
death. What a gladsome trombone the frog
in the wishbone. Is there a question?

The Elk Hunters

They drive their Toyota
& crash it into
the beard of the forest.

The elk head in the truck bed
joins the other heads
& locks horns, as if this
concerto is manufactured.

The jawbone of the timber
mangles the radio first,
now the metal.

Each of the hunters was once
a masticator
of letters, every last one
tenderhearted.

Misplaced

The gypsy moth on
the white cotton shirt
seeks a refuge; my head
a Jupiter that over-
shadows it. Jupiter
hears nothing but alibis
from the pest. My head,
with its Great Red Spot
always on the lookout,
must worry the fated
pariah. Woe, woe, woe,
my birdbrain clucks
like the seraphic hawk
it is, wary marauder.

While Sitting in a Lawn Chair Going Nowhere

I collided with a bumblebee, or was it Saturn, ringed,
humming? Whatever it was, it held the sun, & waywardly
I badmouthed it in the golden hour of the golden day. Here,

there, everywhere,
it denatured the lazy
grass, the heartsease.
If I were to go berserk,
I would not leave
a beauty mark.

The Swimmer, No. 70

The first step is to dive into
the picture & scissor-kick
in a pool of red. There's life
in the red & in silence;
fathomless, unequivocal.
The body is buoyed by red;
where now is Mark Rothko?
He hurts; he can't find his
way out of the pool which is
his expression. A ladder
goes all the way up to Jupiter
unless the body is the ware-
house of transcendence.

Transfused

Yesterday, the Japanese maple in the rain;
the hands—whose were those bloody hands?
Everywhere we went the terrible followed

the beautiful not unlike the suicide of a best friend.
We could do nothing about the blood, which, in another
context, was merciful. Then the rain pushed us back inside

for a Coca-Cola as the leaves indifferently held
the rain. And we forgot about the hands, though
the maple was almost cumbersome with hands.

Suffused

—the half-ton heart of the blue whale. God,
not cowed before the half-ton heart, tells the whale

to intersect a vanishing point, which is the sky
plowed under. And David Hockney says God

may be even greater than a loss of hearing, so as to
sound out the notwithstanding. Wherefore God

bleeds profusely out of the picture in light of
the void, which is the fermata of the half-ton heart.

Emergency on Waxed Paper

Manhattan lies open-
in an automat. It's
O'Hara has admitted
lunch. And yet
offers a nickel slot
receive more blinding
necessary at all times
as O'Hara was
his linen suit, awaiting
watches us stride in
for some change &
may be uncomfortable
we do, that O'Hara's
until we iridesce

faced like a sandwich
the 1950s, & Frank
that he's had enough
the luncheonette
through which one might
light. This makes it
to wear a solar vest,
prone to do, under
the Destroyer. The poet
& ask the counterman
a glass of water. It
to realize, which by now
pencil will fuck with us
like houseflies.

The Cardboard Fawn

While it is living, while it is vital, the cardboard fawn folds itself
at the riverside & takes a drink of manganese water. The legs

bend; they are corrugated. The ears flick; they are tabs. The barcode
on its spine makes the fawn readily identifiable &, when scanned,

distributes it far & wide. These are facts that cannot be disputed.
But perhaps, as one can imagine, the wet lips begin a decimation

that darkens hindquarters & sends the deer downriver into an elegant
collapse, which, in various lights, can look like a wade, swim, or glide.

Waterway

The chandelier in the houseboat is swaying. An unseasonal
snow powders the dock, & a neighbor is shoveling. The house
is as unsteady as it has ever been. My habit is to wait,
as the others wait, sipping coffee, watching
television. What happens in our heads unnerves
us all, but we know that the temperate has an expiration
date. Pieces of ice tumble into the canal as the mooring buckles
& the pontoons of planes drift out into the Sound
that has never in our lifetime frozen. There is one goose,
which for its own reasons, plants its feet at the end
of the dock, & the long black neck with a white chinstrap
draws out of us many false statements, as predicted.

№ 8 Strafes the White-Out

This is a good day. № 8, with her honeysuckle
machine gun, has mowed down the avalanche.

Today we can sleep again, knowing that in hindsight
a cadmium red, in the dead of night a blood orange.

We love № 8, the assassin. The gesso melts;
the whitewash fades. The machine gun nuzzles

the pubic hairs of the forest. There are no alibis
for the green brain, the purple patch, the blue alleluia.

The Interpreter

Loving the antelope that has not yet
come, the caveman goes into the cave
& warms his eyes by the fire. Each thought
is as insipid & flavorless as meat
which has not been arrowed. He wishes
for a salt pile to season the night
& a river to direct the current
of his thirst. But there is nothing
but the noise of the fire & a foregone
conclusion that draws from him
a fluid line. Blue is not present to him;
for though naturally occurring, it
would take millennia to reproduce it,
&, given the earth tones at his feet,
he does not yet dream.

Meantime

We cut off hands to attract the shutterbugs; then
the nightingale flew in.

We cut off feet; more nightingales.

We cut off noses to succor our children; thousands
of nightingales serenaded us.

Whomever we sought to maim, the birds
perched on their stumps.

It was as if the night was a night of golden opportunity.

The nightingales required nothing, & the moon
laid upon us its gold-leaf distinctions.

We were pleased; pretty was as pretty does.

Flush

Beset by cash, the cul-de-sac is sown
with greenbacks. Green, green, unruly color.

Hue that pleasures. Like a mildewed parrot,
the grass will croak, the banknote

will go to seed & become another kind of grenade,
one that euthanizes. Between ochre

& azure, the sod will be taken for a placid
moneyed glade where flamingos clang.

The Earthworms

They hear nothing, wiggling up from the loam
in segments, overcoming their dread

of light. They say nothing to the little ones who
think of themselves as robins, their throats

bassoons, their cocked heads coaxing. Not a
Chopin can wrest from the worms a sonata,

nor can tangents of the clavichord excite them
to noodle. They are impervious to jeremiads.

A paring knife, more or less, elicits surprise;
the smell of rain also gets them writhing. The worms

taste-test earth if the earth is willing. If the clods
are pettifoggers, do the worms absolve them?

№ 8 on Thin Ice

Long after the crystal snowfall, № 8 skates on a pond.
It is not a frozen pond, as now the summer is near

& the blades of her feet cut into water. The mind is murky,
but the skates take № 8 out of the soup, for the blades

are wings, the wings of Mercury. So many secrets № 8
has hid from the dim pond out of which the amphibians

creep. When she looks back at the rink, what strikes her
is the beauty & cunning of her curving. The water

is plausible though far from clean or translucent. To №
8, whether feigned or authentic, the pond seems verdant.

Self-Portrait

The womb of personality
deploys in faraway regions where a mantis
crawls out of a mayonnaise jar. The field
is knee-high, grassy; my pajamas
are covered with aircraft; & someone is
playing a toy piano under a jet
stream. The first notes are relevant for, if
I find myself

      strapping down a helicopter
on the deck of a carrier, the chopper
is called a Tiger, which is also
a Swallowtail. The mother who brought me
here & clothed me in winged things
wishes for more than, equal to, less than.

Second Person

You escape your childhood a Confederate
spy. Instructions you don't understand
& intended for someone you don't know
are typed on a tape that is coiled in the heel
of your shoe. The tunnel under your bedroom
leads out into the prison yard, & from
there you scale a wall, steal a horse, jump a train.
A race toward confidants can only
take you so far. You decide to head back
into the solitary confinement
of better days & follow the river
that suns itself like a Copperhead. At last
you arrive where you first conspired; but the snake-
skin in your shoe, for whom? And what
of the plot underfoot? Underwritten?

Hardship

The gardener hits the deer in the head
with a shovel, & the deer, stunned, takes
a step forward then tumbles into
the embrace of the gardener, & the gardener,
unsure, lets go of the implement & grabs
the animal around the neck & feels a gasp
coming up through the neck, & the breath
which is wet strikes him on the cheek; together
they fall into a bed of jonquils, & there they lie
for the better part of a lifetime, the surprising
weight of the deer pressing harder & harder
into the embrace, & the gardener beside himself
stroking the speckled hide & calling out
for someone, anyone, to peel back the scalp
& inject a memory of himself as he once was,
selfish, without a bedfellow.

Miró

In the beginning, there is the sun.
Then the eye of a mule. These are
followed by a tree, which looks so much
like a guitar that the Spaniard, also in the scene,

believes that the tree *is* a guitar, & yet it
surprises him that the tree, on which he plays, is not
terrified of stroke, as he is, & more so
because beguiled.

The mule stamps its feet; this is what mules
do when mules think they are going
somewhere.

Photosensitive

My skull, my reef
where the brain coral
blooms; starfish
migrate to a hue
of me.

My name
is also Dry
Land; I capture
Red Rock in bone
marrow. One

day I step into dead
leaves, one night
the anemone. What-
ever necrosis is
it cleans my clock.

Pelvis Series

There has been no touching the whole way here.
Where are your puzzle pieces? Why are

they out looking for other puzzles? You can see the gambol
of the forlorn in the June bug; it hovers over the Sinai peninsula

of our pelvises.
It turns clumsily
from the rosebush,
the twilight.

A Moral Color

Under the yonder, I searched for my name in a blue
book. The pages were doors without knobs or keyholes, yet,

because blue comforts the eyes, the tome opened up to me.
Suddenly I had a taste for blue; it depicted the impossible.

For both Greeks & Romans there was no blue in the rainbow,
but here, by sunlight, the most audacious sapphire. And so

I forsook the allure of verdigris, cochineal, & mulberry
& walked to the river where, having polluted the water, the dyers

waited for it to clear. Rather than tinctures, a miraculous
draft of fishes came up with their buckets. But this was

not the end, nor the beginning, of my faraway look away.

The Carnivores

[1]Then Jesus took off his sugarcoat
& walked into the wild

like an aborigine; [2]there he met beast after beast
that beheld him. And he

countermanded them, turning their appetites
into his flesh. [3]Their tongues,

reconstituted as deviled meat,
he stored under the roof of his mouth; [4]for he spoke

in parables. The hyena, caked
in blood, [5]dreamed of a wedding cake.

A Discovery Said to Fail

It must be
we are snow-blind, all
asterisks, no Anchor. Had we
been lighthearted, we would have loved
light, its heaviness. About the whale in the guitar
case, the white whale, the blankness, & how the singsong
version of snow in which we compose ourselves has been put away,
let us levitate. The whale, breaching, intermittent as lighthouse, is long-
ways laid in yesterday's whaler: ponderous, noisome avalanche: battleship.

Weightless in the Void a Friend Went Dark

Because a friend took her life & in doing so
made me a stranger, I became an astronaut.

The astronaut in straying from the failsafe
takes into space a lifeline. Whereas the suicidal

friend sundered without. What she thought in the dark
never reached me nor did it coincide. Today,

the columbine opens to a bombardment
of photons; if this is light. Whereas the astronaut

spacewalks. It has a reason, this absence of light;
I carry a manufactured light with me.

My friend did not open like the columbine,
whose petals are spurs, crimson in the cutthroat of light.

Reading Edward Taylor

A neon fog
floats out of the mouth
of the incinerator;

a piebald snowfall
beclouds the mind
like a library.

To be alive is to feel
the pulp of your
tongue between

bicuspids.
Or to glut the acid-
free pages of earth

with "Garbag'd
deer" & "Heaven's
Sugar Cake."

The Estrangement

At noon I eat light, the light
of the world; in the evening I eat a sailboat
with its spinnaker full of last bits.

The rudder turns my heart, &, leaving behind a buoy, a line, an anchor,
I drift over the surface of what could be linseed oil.

I am the same as a loon, a paintbrush
calling for paint. Thickly I comprehend all languages
including the keel

that holds me upright. The star field above the hillside dotes upon the ironclad
colors of the insomniac, yet

in this space, faced with immediate
danger, one cannot help asking again for the invisible.

Poem for Hans Arp

I love you, Hans Arp, aiming your rocket launcher
at a cloud. The cloud

comes down breathless like a pearl diver,
as the sun, over easy, serene, blesses the weevils. Hans Arp,

when you dabble among them, making a quodlibet of every
living thing, I want to touch the carbuncle

of your burst wound. Should this happen, & certainly
it will, the sea will follow you into the tall, tall cotton, torn & pasted.

The Derelict

A dire young man finds a cello. He bobs up & down
with the warp of it; he is sprawled over the wreck of it.

He is fed (clouds scud, winds menace) by a few stalks of cane
that sugar his lips as he saws at the nethermost strings.

From where comes the cane? From the silt inside the cello.
The silt is quartz & feldspar; it looks like all the sand

of the sphinx. It proves to the castaway that the cello
cannot be embittered if it is as it once was.

№ 8 Keeps Her Word

№ 8 feels close to the glass man
who is not threatening, not threatening

unless jagged, not jagged if transparent,
if aquamarine. № 8 can see her breath

on the glass man; she knows what she's said
& to whom it matters. № 8 withdraws to

the orange tree in the orange grove, & there is
the glass man among the chartreuse nebula.

Seeing the glass man in the darkness, seeing
the glassy sea of him, № 8 is mesmerized

by the manner of him, by the invisible
door through which she enters him.

The Lost Chord

A police boat
anchors like a tractor
in a meadow. It is
inevitable, the flamingo
in the guitar strings
of the sea, not as
pink as imagined
but astonishingly
supple, appealing,
the neck integral
to the inquest.

This is what you
fear when waking
alone in the dark,
the strangulation.
Now the air-horn
sounds when you
could have held
that neck as
the guitarist did
with the dragnet
of her hand.

46

Blowing My Horn

It was a time when Jesus wanted me to be more
than Little Boy Blue.

I had an unfortunate middle-of-the-road
attitude that led me to sleepwalk
with an ax. A history

of nodding off meant I butchered
the constellations. Under
all that fluorescence came a shock wave, then a Milky

Way. A blur, the face of Christ, as I milked
my horn—less moonbeam
than haymaker where the sun don't shine.

Then, as now, it seemed a shame to dismember the peace. So
I went around the world in a combine
looking for Jesus.

A siren, which in ancient times wrecked Iowa,
was always up before morning light.

Hearsay

The mailman sent piecemeal a rare donkey
to the city of waters; to the city of waters
a rare donkey was sent, swaddled
in blueprint.

And it came to pass that the waters
were troubled. Woe
in the great city.

Nothing is more beautiful than to admit
the truth, or more difficult.

The head & tail & all that is in between.

When piecemeal the beast was sent,
the engineers knew their place.

For if disassembled like a boat
the rare donkey could be
put together.

But to separate the members of a living
thing, to cast dispersions on it,
this is to create a question
unanswerable.

The Memory Is Spotted with Fire

You wait in the garden for the ineffable
on a balmy night. You are not so bluff
as to intimidate, not like Marblehead that swallows
the high tide. A southerly rainstorm has swept
through the neighborhood; a rabbit pauses in the wet
grass under the chestnut tree & holds a mirror
in its front feet. You are thinking
of Concord, the mind that agrees with everything,
the swift pace of the afterlife. How is it that
your brain, emulsified, cannot remember
the names? This much is apparent: the past
is glossy enough to look through, the night
slapdash with leaps.

Feign of Frogs

I want the frogs, right as rain, the green atmosphere
of peculiar things. The green man, if it snows on him,

it snows from nowhere blue. I play the gold banjo;
I play it loud until doubtless gold. I lose my trove in syrinx

& the throaty. The rain believes; it is a day of syringes;
laud be flimsy as goldenrod. Say feckless;

say the mouth regales; say frogs & the green man
& whoops-a-daisy. Right as rain; green as peculiar.

The Hydrangea

In a hospital bed, the hydrangea
lies sedated. A gown covers it,
stem to neck, but neglects sunburned ankles
that seem to have walked a mile through dune grass.
What a day that must have been, the head
of the flower, in a bathing cap, out
searching for wavy blue. June, the blooming
season, greenhouse of panicles & Starstreaks.
August, rainwater dripping through a
French horn of tubes, the hydrangea
dishevels on a pillow, wilted giant.

Night, Idaho, Faraway Meadow

My eyes are on the see-through cows standing in a petticoat of moonshine.
Behind them, the hyacinths spiral out-of-control, such that the bovines

turn purple. Clarity has its drawbacks, but in this case the Plain-
Jane cattle become pastoral in a new sense: sacredly they preside

over the clearing. By speaking in this way, I may mutilate them,
but more likely what I see will be what I get. My lips leer at the foment

of udders & the psychedelic motions of the various stomachs,
& as yet I have no snow machine to safekeep the way of all flesh.

Wright

There is a Frank
Lloyd Wright
growing out of
my rib cage,

a concrete slab cantilevered over the shady slope
of my timbers. I am not afraid of the starry sky

that walks. Nor
the one-winged
flicker. Though
it feels as if
my footprint
has been
fabricated, it
also is a wing.

Los Angeles

Take us to the saffron hills, the angelfish
in swimming pools, a graveyard.

And mark for us the Lepidoptera, the 88s
that have strayed from South America

& which seem to be asking a series
of astronomical questions. Why, dazed

by our pleasures, would we acknowledge
wishes that are wilder than our left hands?

The weather, so people say, has changed
our opinion about the fiery end of cities.

But when we ride in our tricked out,
two-door Eldorado, it is praiseworthy

to bury one another in song; in
the same way, we become superlative.

Mortified

And standing at the sink, I squeeze a tube & brush
my teeth with forsythia. My yellow teeth are seed corn

I will plant in rows, bedside. Come morning, the ears
will be loaded on a train that makes mincemeat of train
tracks. Eyes, nose, set aside. So, as blue lips are the only

thing left of my face, forget this smile impossibly
placid on which I sail the newsprint of a paper boat.

Architecture Acts Slowly, If at All

From under a bridge, a man cries out
in his makeshift; the wings of this man are nicked; the eagle
cannot quarter or harbor. The skyscraper on the fault line
is as curvy as the backbone of a camel; it's painful
for the dromedary to offer its delicious hump. The infinite lies down
in the middle of the city, but, while the abstract wants
to be known as a lover, the concrete can't help
but remain aloft, beautifully
sculptured.

Same Sun, Same Stars, Same Father

Not far from the ziggurat at Ur, two soldiers
carry a heron between them. This is my father
being swung like a sack of slate.

Every day he used to work the blackboard;
now he is ashen. I will never let his umbrageous
feathers be harvested for a flying machine,

even if that machine aspires to dervish, even
if the wings, though brittle, miraculously
convey the outlines of history. For the chalk

of his bones could just as well blaspheme.
The dearth of the man remains in the mind,
a wading bird of what & how within forever.

California

Haystacks post the way to heaven. There are not many gold-
brickers who live here among the bales; mostly pilgrims. But beyond the fields,
pears begin to nipple

in the orchard that is forbidden. You can't photograph pears
without also blowing them up, as now they are mere larva. I suppose this means
that hashmallim

have visited the trees. Somehow when you climb over the hill
& into the pasture where sheep have slept away whole afternoons you're dazzled:
this earth is more

than a pale blue dot as the astrophysicist claims. And beyond,
in a second pasture, the whale coaxes delirium from his swarm of krill. See?
The cow let out

of the barn will cross the road & eventually pacify the minutes
you've loved. If there are 8 such cows in the landscape, spare the earth its
pale blue attributes.

The Nuclear Age

Underneath its wings, the robin
wears a hazmat suit.

Sincerely
the robin swallows a catchphrase
as the head pivots.

Home, a few long strands of grass
that coax the sky.

The typewriter
is dead. It can't help thinking
how, nested in ribbon,

it hammered out the fault-
line of a blue egg.

Woman in the Sun, 1961

I say to the woman: true, you are alive;
you stand perpendicular to the plinth of light
with a cigarette in your hand & shoes under
the unmade bed & the sun asserting itself on grassy

dunes. It must not
be necessary for you
to wear clothes;
your disregard &
doe-eyed breasts
better express your
attitude toward
the light that warms
you. So in your
birthday suit you
enter feet first,
cadaver on a slab
at the crematorium.
You begin as mote;
you advance as
particles of Flake
White pigment
suspended in oil;
you end as
matter-of-fact.

One Whose Soul the Titan Has Fashioned

The brain fails; brain, why do you fail? For in idealizing
the footprints of William Howard Taft among the cow pies,

& undoubtedly he must have walked in pastures, you must sense
that he is no longer with us, that enormous man, our largest

president, who nevertheless stands the test of time, for here
you are with outsized footnotes that have tracked across

the Internet. A multitude of endangered animals have left
similar traces on stamp collections owned by gods not fleas.

№ 7 Builds a Bomb

In the end, it is not a matter of the unpredictable.
№ 7 is familiar with the device, the sum of its parts,

which under the sun a hothouse makes. And bright as he is,
it is not as if he can devise otherwise; the giant

that shadows his steps follows him to the bottomlessness
of his undertaker's pace. Omens boom. № 7 abstracts.

He himself out of the blue synthetic pitter-patter
tintinnabulates without a time signature.

Grant Wood

The father looks out of a gothic window
that opens to a railway; the rails cut through
oaks into a clearing. The deer there feed on

electric grass as if
a fable in the placid
scene. The boy milking
the cows in the barn is
no more a milk snake
than first man on the
moon, but his aversion
to the picturesque is
a picture in itself.

Worrisome Bird

The yellowthroat laments the big bang; the upshot
is that, as star shrapnel, the bird has a ways to go.

The on-again, off-again phrasing of the warbler is felt as raindrops.

Thunder overwhelms all of it; the lightning,
catalyst, widespread over an orchard, cannot pinpoint
which note is in which place at which time.

So be it; there is need for a yellowthroat as warped as a Bosc pear.

The Spaniards

Absent-minded & unapproachable, I walk
in the tilled field. I am not, in fact, here;
I am only anticipating the Catalan farm
& a lane of carob trees. A butterfly wing
produces a shock, as does a sardine tin
& the unattainable sea that is at eye-level.
I listen for the dialogue of insects
& the whimper of a rabbit that is held
by the ears by a peasant woman. She is nude
except for her cyclopean hips, which are true
& false the way the bone of the moon is not yet
blue, not yet superlative. What makes the scene
real is the mule-drawn cart that disappears
in a cloud of dust, just as turpentine
erases forkfuls of sunshine from my mouth.

The Bystanders

A dead fox in the forest; young George Washington espies it. He
gets off his horse, an invisible horse, & inspects the orange & cream-
colored loins of the fox which has expired like the April snow
in a bed of pine needles. He pauses as if for a portrait, & when the sun
hits his head he seems to be crowned with a jeweled miter. In a few short
months, he will be reaching for a rose, & later someone will call him "the urchin,"
& later still a compatriot will dismantle his mouth & hold up his tooth
with tongs. The real but invisible horse joins a few indistinct cows that,
following their own code of conduct, have wandered away
from the homestead. Above, floating on clouds, the bystanders.

The Spectator

I, King Rat, lie in the hibiscus of my own blood. It is the Year
of the Rat. The hibiscus blooms; the paramedic Life-

Flight hovers above me; I hear the whistle of the referee. I suppose
I wandered across a field painted with lines & was struck by

the cleat of a lineman. I suppose, at midfield, I now sing out
to the Rat Pack because I's a dirty rat & I's not dodged the mob.

My blood is lukewarm; the sky-cam catches me prone; the bleachers
give way to a high-rise where I once lived catastrophically above it all.

Ping

A woman with a tin ear
listens for her own voice. She wades into gorse
& looks out at herring boats in the North Sea. There
is no name for the child that will not be born
to her, & the wind undermines her
intention to hear it. How did
she get here & where is
the auk that builds
its nest in the
cavity of the
wind? It's
easy to
imagine a
siren in the
rubble by the sea
or to think of the
woman as a submarine.

The Physician

Today might be the day of an aortic
aneurysm, yet the fox plays in periwinkle
& the ballpoint blue of the lake is for sailing.

The sail collapses like a lung; the fox plays
on. The periwinkle gives way
to star traffic, & the boats are in transit.

When they flatline, there is a vacancy
with which to make do. Like the blank check
of the prescription pad. And the day ends.

Meditation, No. 70

You are eating a peach poolside
when wing-nuts drop into the water;

   a little later come tailfins,
   blades, skids, chassis, rotors,
   then a canopy like the head
   of a hippopotamus.

A helicopter, disembodied, has pitched itself
out of the blue into the blue;

   you have merely opened
   the space of a peach pit.

Happy in the Hard Saying

Thank you
for this peninsula cocooned in rocks. You satisfy me
in the Northwest & also my father
who was farsighted.
The coastline does not heal
all wounds. There are mudslides that slur
the Pacific, the Pacific
where the brine is blue & the whales are humpbacks.
Yet when is a wave not a hindsight?
Sea planes follow the latitude of their instruments
except when flying blind;
wherever the little crosses are going, I am happy
with my wings of burnt toast.

Penultimate

The pond is heavy with snow; craters sink in the whiteness; perhaps a rhinoceros
on a hillock, perhaps something imperceptible, something on the margins,
has come & gone. The asteroid

leaves few tracks, but it could have been an asteroid, farfetched, looking to graze;
the snow radiates a dull pain. Falling, if only a little, the snowflakes pave
the pond on which the numinous soft-shoes. Therefore,
somewhere, a laugh.

Magnificat

If God died suddenly, not God but a tiger in a snowfield, not
a snowfield, an ice-storm; what would God say/ about a tiger

in an ice-storm? The neighborhood newly turned to glass has seen
a hunter/ on his knees, a hunter in an orange cap with/ a flask

of Maker's/ Mark. There is hardly anything killed/ that does not
live again; the tiger/ by the scruff of its neck is borne in the mouth

of God, God/ with ultraviolet stripes that are the wounds of
generations. The ice-laden/ elms, whose limbs bear the Emerald

Ash Borer, are on fire now & again because of/ sunbursts; unexpected each breath that surpasses breath; thus, enough said.

Notes

"Intrepid Pilot" invokes the Spanish and Mexican artist Remedios Varo and grifts some of its images from Janet A. Kaplan's *Remedios Varo: Unexpected Journeys.*

The existential question "Is life worth living?" foregrounded in "Sanctuary" is succinctly expressed by the American philosopher and psychologist William James.

"Dooms of Balm" is a phrase that originates in the Emily Dickinson poem "Opon a Lilac Sea" (1368).

The first sentence in "Knickerbocker" is borrowed from a hypothetical posed by N. T. Wright in *Surprised by Hope: Rethinking Heaven, the Resurrection, and the Mission of the Church.*

"Painters on Our Way to Work" modifies the title of one of Vincent Van Gogh's paintings. The first lines of the poem compress a statement by the American painter Grant Wood. Wood said, "Almost all of us have some dream power in our childhood, but without encouragement it leaves us and then we become bored and tired and ordinary. In most of our studies, we deal only with material things or in ideas that are materialistic. We are carefully coached in the most modern and efficient ways of making our bodies comfortable and we become so busy about getting ourselves all nicely placed that we are apt to forget the dream spirit that is born in all of us. Then someday, when we are physically comfortable, we remember dimly a distant land we used to visit in our youth. We try to go again but we cannot find the way. Our imagination machinery is withered just as our legs or arms might wither if we forget for years and years to use them."

"Figure at Night Following Phosphorescent Tracks" takes its title and its inception from a painting by Joan Miró.

"The Swimmer, No. 70" responds to Mark Rothko, who in 1970 was discovered dead in his Manhattan studio, his arms slashed with a razor.

The line attributed to David Hockney in "Suffused" is altered; Hockney actually said, "God must be even greater than we dreamed."

"Meantime" is inspired by Philip Gourevitch's 2010 investigative piece in *The New Yorker* called "Alms Dealers."

"The Earthworms" interacts with passages from Charles Darwin's 1881 treatise *The Formation of Vegetable Mould through the Action of Worms, with Observations on Their Habits.*

"Second Person" derives from an account of the 1863 escape of John Hunt Morgan from the Ohio Penitentiary, told by James D. Horan in *Confederate Agent. A Discovery in History* (1954); my great-grandfather Boswell Partlow Yates Gorham, as family lore describes it, served Morgan and his Raiders as a surgeon.

"Pelvis Series" appropriates its title from the Georgia O'Keefe series of paintings, which she began in 1943.

"A Moral Color" renovates information from Michel Pastoureau's *Blue: The History of a Color.*

The title "A Discovery Said to Fail" is lifted from a line of Herman Melville's: "It is my earnest desire to write those sorts of books that are said to fail." The poem also drafts off of William James, who said more fully, "How has the gospel been so misunderstood? If obscure, how is the possession of such a dark thing an advantage? It must be that we have a native blindness."

"Hearsay" hearkens back to legends told in *The Histories* by Herodotus.

"The Memory Is Spotted with Fire" manipulates a line by Ralph Waldo Emerson in "The Divinity School Address": "...the meadow is spotted with fire and gold in the tint of flowers." The poem recasts a scene in which William and Henry James visit the home of the elderly Emerson, who by this time suffers from aphasia.

"Woman in the Sun, 1961" responds to the painting of the same name by Edward Hopper.

"One Whose Soul the Titan Has Fashioned" discovers its title in a line from Montaigne quoted by Ralph Waldo Emerson in his journals.

"Grant Wood" depends upon James Dennis's volume: *Grant Wood. A Study in American Art and Culture.*

"The Spaniards" plunders language from art essays on the Catalan painter Joan Miró.

"The Bystanders" imports imagery viewed at the Frick Art Museum in Manhattan.

Acknowledgments

The author gratefully acknowledges the following magazines in which poems from the book first appeared:

"California," "St. Francis," "Ping," & "Blowing My Horn" in *Denver Quarterly*; "Waterway" in *The Cincinnati Review*; "Transfused" in *Copper Nickel*; "Hearsay" in *Arts & Academe*; "The Head of George Washington" & "Figure at Night Following Phosphorescent Tracks" in *Hotel Amerika*; "Meantime" & "Architecture Acts Slowly, If at All" in *jubilat*; "Intrepid Pilot" in *Columbia: A Journal of Literature and Art*; "The Swimmer, No. 70" in *Washington Square*; "Second Person," "Hardship," "Knickerbocker," & "Same Sun, Same Stars, Same Father" in *West Branch*; "Painters on Our Way to Work," "The Hydrangea," & "While Sitting in a Lawn Chair Going Nowhere" in *New Orleans Review*; "St. Louis & "The "Spaniards" in *Colorado Review*; "Penultimate" in *Black Tongue Review*; "The Cardboard Fawn" in *Indiana Review*; "A Moral Color" in *Blackbird*; "One Whose Soul the Titan Has Fashioned" in *Narrative*; "Miró" in *Columbia Poetry Review*; "The Elk Hunters" in *Bateau*; "Night, Idaho, Faraway Meadow" in *BOMB*; "Sanctuary" in *Ghost Town*; "№ 8 Strafes the White-Out," "№ 8 on Thin Ice," & "№ 8 Keeps Her Word" in *Wag's Revue*; "The Carnivores" & "The Estrangement" in *The Cresset*; "A Discovery Said to Fail" in *VOLT*; "Suffused" & "Emergency on Waxed Paper" in *The Iowa Review*; "Magnificat" in *Harvard Review*.

The author wishes to express gratitude to the editors of *Verse Daily* and *Poetry Daily* for featuring his poems on their websites.

The author is thankful for the editorial and design work of Don Hettinga, David Blakesley, and Jon Thompson.

The author also offers his appreciation to Calvin College's Alumni Association, Dean for Research and Scholarship, and Dean for Arts, Languages, & Education for course releases and travel funds that made this book possible.

About the Author

L. S. Klatt's first book, *Interloper*, was awarded the Juniper Prize for Poetry and was published by the University of Massachusetts Press in 2009. His second collection, *Cloud of Ink*, won the Iowa Poetry Prize and came out from the University of Iowa Press in 2011. His lyric poem "Andrew Wyeth, Painter, Dies At 91" was anthologized in *Best American Poetry 2011* and subsequently made into a ninety-second animated film. He is the current Poet Laureate of Grand Rapids, Michigan.

Photo of the author by Jason Glerum. Used by permission

Free Verse Editions

Edited by Jon Thompson

13 ways of happily by Emily Carr
Between the Twilight and the Sky by Jennie Neighbors
Blood Orbits by Ger Killeen
The Bodies by Chris Sindt
The Book of Isaac by Aidan Semmens
Canticle of the Night Path by Jennifer Atkinson
Child in the Road by Cindy Savett
Condominium of the Flesh by Valerio Magrelli, translated by Clarissa
    Botsford
Contrapuntal by Christopher Kondrich
Country Album by James Capozzi
The Curiosities by Brittany Perham
Current by Lisa Fishman
Dismantling the Angel by Eric Pankey
Divination Machine by F. Daniel Rzicznek
Erros by Morgan Lucas Schuldt
The Forever Notes by Ethel Rackin
The Flying House by Dawn-Michelle Baude
Instances: Selected Poems by Jeongrye Choi, translated by Brenda
    Hillman, Wayne de Fremery, and Jeongrye Choi
The Magnetic Bracket by Jesús Losada, translated by Luis Ingelmo and
    Michael Smith
A Map of Faring by Peter Riley
No Shape Bends the River So Long by Monica Berlin and Beth Marzoni
Pilgrimly by Siobhan Scarry
Physis by Nicolas Pesque, translated by Cole Swensen
Poems from above the Hill & Selected Work by Ashur Etwebi, translated
    by Brenda Hillman and Diallah Haidar
The Prison Poems by Miguel Hernández, translated by Michael Smith
Puppet Wardrobe by Daniel Tiffany
Quarry by Carolyn Guinzio
remanence by Boyer Rickel
Signs Following by Ger Killeen
Split the Crow by Sarah Sousa
Summoned by Guillevic, translated by Monique Chefdor
Sunshine Wound by L. S. Klatt

These Beautiful Limits by Thomas Lisk
An Unchanging Blue: Selected Poems 1962–1975 by Rolf Dieter
    Brinkmann, translated by Mark Terrill
Under the Quick by Molly Bendall
Verge by Morgan Lucas Schuldt
The Wash by Adam Clay
We'll See by George Godeau, translated by Kathleen McGookey
What Stillness Illuminated by Yermiyahu Ahron Taub
Winter Journey [Viaggio d'inverno] by Attilio Bertolucci, translated by
    Nicholas Benson
Wonder Rooms by Allison Funk

CPSIA information can be obtained
at www.ICGtesting.com
Printed in the USA
FFOW04n1128160115
10240FF